HIGH FIBRE
COOKBOOK

Consultant Editor:
Valerie Ferguson

LORENZ BOOKS

Contents

Introduction

Dietary fibre, or non-starch polysaccharides (NSP) as it is more accurately called, plays an essential part in a properly balanced diet. It is important for maintaining a healthy digestive system and in the prevention of heart disease and certain cancers. The average amount of fibre eaten is 11–13 grams per day, although the recommended daily intake is between 12–18 grams.

It is very easy to increase the fibre content of your meals by simply replacing refined ingredients with unrefined ones or by adding extra beans, fruit or vegetables to dishes. It is worth keeping a stock of high fibre ingredients in your store cupboard – brown rice, canned and dried beans, peas and lentils, oats, seeds, wholemeal flour and wholewheat pasta. A good supply of fresh fruit and vegetables not only increases the fibre in the diet, but also provides important vitamins and minerals.

All the tempting and nutritious recipes in this book contain a minimum of 4 grams of fibre per serving. There is also useful information on increasing fibre in your diet. This is your first important step to increased health, vitality and general well-being.

High Fibre Eating

High Fibre Diet for Life

While it is easy to change to a diet that is higher in fibre, it should be done gradually, as sudden changes to your eating patterns can upset your digestive system. For example, use a mixture of white and wholemeal flours when you first introduce fibre into your diet.

There are many more ways of increasing the fibre in your diet than simply adding bran. In fact, wheat bran can be an irritant and contains a substance called phytate, which may interfere with the absorption of minerals. If you choose foods that are naturally high in fibre, you will also benefit from other important nutrients in those foods. Simply switching from white to wholemeal bread, white pasta to wholewheat pasta, white rice to brown rice or choosing wholewheat breakfast cereals, are easy ways of gradually introducing more fibre into your diet.

Add dried fruit, such as raisins, chopped, ready-to-eat dried pears or peaches, to breakfast cereals or porridge. Extend soups by adding cooked pulses, such as beans, peas or lentils. Add grated root vegetables to casseroles, stews and sauces. Use wholemeal breadcrumbs in stuffings, coatings and toppings.

Avoid peeling fruit and vegetables whenever possible, but always wash them thoroughly. Potatoes are especially delicious cooked in their skins – whether baked, boiled or even roasted.

Serve pulse-based dishes as a change from meat- or fish-based ones. Choose fresh or dried fruit salad or compote, wholemeal bread pudding, wholemeal crumbles or fruit cakes for dessert. Serve wholemeal bread, rolls, pitta bread or toast with each meal.

Make sandwiches using wholemeal, wholegrain or Granary bread, and snack on fresh or dried fruit.

High Fibre Food Chart

The information shows dietary fibre in grams per 100 g/3½ oz of foodstuff.

	Fibre (g)
Breads	
brown	3.5
Granary	4.3
white	1.5
white with added fibre	3.1
wholemeal	5.8
wholemeal pitta	6.4

Breakfast cereals	
All-bran	24.5
Branflakes	13.0
Cornflakes	0.9
Fruit 'n' Fibre	7.0
muesli (no added sugar)	7.6
Ready Brek	7.2
Shredded Wheat	9.8
Weetabix	9.7

Flours & grains	
brown rice, boiled	0.8
porridge oats	7.0
wheat bran	36.4
wheat flour, white	3.1
wheat flour, wholemeal	9.0
white rice, boiled	0.1
white pasta, boiled	1.2
wholemeal pasta, boiled	3.5

Fruit	
(Figures given are for raw fruit unless otherwise stated)	
apple, eating	1.8
avocado	3.4
banana	1.1
figs, dried	6.9
gooseberries, stewed, no sugar	2.0
grapefruit	1.3
mango	2.5
orange	1.7
peach	1.5
peaches, dried	7.3
pear	2.2
pears, dried	8.3
pineapple	1.2
prunes	5.7
raisins	2.0
sultanas	2.0

Nuts & seeds	
almonds	7.4
brazil nuts	4.3
desiccated coconut	13.7
hazelnuts	6.5
peanuts	6.2
pistachio nuts	6.1
pumpkin seeds	5.3
sesame seeds	7.9

Pastry	
shortcrust, cooked	2.2
wholemeal shortcrust, cooked	6.3

Pulses	
baked beans in tomato sauce	3.7
butter beans, canned	4.6
chick-peas, canned	4.1
lentils, brown and green, boiled	3.8
lentils, red split, boiled	1.9
mangetouts, boiled	2.2
peas, boiled	5.1
red kidney beans	6.2

Vegetables	
broccoli, boiled	2.3
Brussels sprouts, boiled	3.1
cabbage, boiled	1.8
carrots, boiled	2.5
leeks, boiled	1.7
onion, raw	1.4
parsnips, boiled	4.7
potatoes, baked in skins	2.7
spinach, raw	2.1
spring greens, boiled	2.6
sweet potatoes, boiled	2.3
sweetcorn kernels, canned	1.4
turnips, boiled	1.9

Useful Techniques

Preparing Pulses

To destroy potentially harmful toxins, most pulses need to be rapidly boiled, uncovered for 10 minutes. The heat should then be reduced to a simmer for the rest of the cooking time.

1 Pick out any small stones or discoloured peas or beans and rinse the pulses in cold running water.

3 A quicker alternative is to put the dried beans or peas in a large pan of water, bring to the boil and boil for 2 minutes, then leave them to soak for 1 hour. Drain and rinse well.

4 In either case, drain the pulses and rinse them well. They are now ready for cooking according to the recipe.

2 Put dried beans or peas in a bowl, cover with cold water and soak for at least 4 hours. (Lentils do not need soaking.) Drain and rinse well.

5 Put the soaked and drained beans or peas, or the lentils, in a pan of fresh cold water (3 parts water to 1 part pulses) and bring to the boil. Boil for 10 minutes, cover, reduce the heat and simmer until tender. Do not add salt during cooking as it will toughen the skins.

Cooking Long Grain Brown Rice

1 Put the rice in a large saucepan and cover with boiling water (about 1.4 litres/2¼ pints/5¾ cups of water to 250 g/9 oz/1⅓ cups rice). Stir, bring back to the boil and simmer, uncovered, for about 35 minutes, until tender but still slightly chewy.

2 Drain the rice through a fine sieve, then rinse it with fresh boiling water to remove some of the sticky starch.

Making Wholemeal Shortcrust Pastry

1 Put the wholemeal flour and salt in a bowl and add the fat. Rub it into the flour with your fingertips until the mixture resembles breadcrumbs. Using a round-bladed knife, stir in small amounts of cold water until the mixture begins to stick together.

2 Collect the dough together and knead lightly to form a smooth, soft ball. Cover and leave to rest in the fridge for 30 minutes before using.

Minestrone

A glorious mixture of pulses, fresh vegetables and pasta, this classic peasant soup is healthy, filling and completely delicious.

Serves 6–8

INGREDIENTS
30 ml/2 tbsp olive oil
50 g/2 oz smoked streaky
    bacon, diced
2 large onions, chopped
2 garlic cloves, crushed
2 medium carrots, diced
3 celery sticks, sliced
225 g/8 oz/1¼ cups dried haricot beans,
    soaked in cold water and drained
400 g/14 oz can chopped tomatoes
2.5 litres/4 pints/10 cups
    beef stock
350 g/12 oz potatoes, diced
175 g/6 oz/1½ cups small pasta shapes
    (such as macaroni, stars, shells)
225 g/8 oz/2 cups green cabbage,
    thinly sliced
175 g/6 oz/1 cup fine green
    beans, sliced
115 g/4 oz/1 cup frozen peas
45 ml/3 tbsp chopped fresh parsley
salt and freshly ground
    black pepper
freshly grated Parmesan cheese,
    to serve

1 Heat the olive oil in a large saucepan and add the diced bacon, chopped onions and crushed garlic. Cover and cook gently, stirring occasionally, for 5 minutes, until the onions begin to soften.

2 Add the carrots and celery to the bacon mixture and cook for 2–3 minutes, until softening.

3 Add the drained beans to the pan with the chopped tomatoes and stock. Bring to the boil, then reduce the heat. Cover and simmer for 2–2½ hours, until the beans are tender.

VARIATION: To make *Soupe au Pistou* from the South of France, stir in a basil, garlic and pine nut sauce (pesto or pistou) just before serving.

4 Add the potatoes 30 minutes before the soup is finished. Add the pasta, cabbage, beans, peas and parsley 15 minutes before the soup is ready. Season to taste and serve with a bowl of freshly grated Parmesan cheese.

Lentil Soup with Tomatoes

High in fibre and protein-rich, lentils do not have a strong flavour so they are perfect combined with other stronger-tasting ingredients.

Serves 4

INGREDIENTS
45 ml/3 tbsp extra virgin olive oil
3 rindless streaky bacon rashers, cut into
    small dice
1 onion, finely chopped
2 celery sticks, finely chopped
2 carrots, finely diced
2 rosemary sprigs, finely chopped
2 bay leaves
225 g/8 oz/1 cup dried green or brown lentils
400 g/14 oz can plum tomatoes
1.75 litres/3 pints/7½ cups
    vegetable stock
salt and freshly ground black pepper
bay leaves and rosemary sprigs, to garnish

2 Tip in the tomatoes and stock and bring to the boil. Lower the heat, half cover the pan, and simmer for about 1 hour, or until the lentils are tender.

3 Remove the bay leaves, add salt and pepper to taste and serve with a garnish of fresh bay leaves and rosemary sprigs.

COOK'S TIP: If you are unused to eating pulses and are concerned you will find them indigestible, lentils are a good pulse to try as they are more easily digested than larger beans. Look out for the small green lentils in quality groceries or delicatessens. Store all pulses in airtight containers in a cool, dry and dark place.

1 Heat the oil in a large saucepan. Add the bacon and cook for about 3 minutes, then stir in the onion and cook for 5 minutes, until softened. Stir in the prepared celery, carrots, rosemary, bay leaves and lentils. Toss over the heat for 1 minute, until thoroughly coated in the oil.

Pasta & Chick-pea Soup

Like all pulses, chick-peas are a valuable source of dietary fibre and complex carbohydrates. They also have a wonderful nutty flavour which is enhanced by bacon and garlic in this substantial soup.

Serves 4–6

INGREDIENTS
200 g/7 oz/1 cup dried chick-peas,
   soaked overnight in cold water
   and drained
3 garlic cloves
1 bay leaf
90 ml/6 tbsp olive oil
50 g/2 oz/⅓ cup bacon, diced
1 sprig fresh rosemary, plus extra to garnish
600 ml/1 pint/2½ cups water
150 g/5 oz ditalini or other short
   hollow pasta
salt and freshly ground black pepper

2 Simmer, adding more water as necessary, for about 2 hours, until tender. Remove the bay leaf. Pass about half the chick-peas through a food mill or process in a food processor with a few tablespoons of the cooking liquid. Return the purée to the pan with the rest of the chick-peas and the remaining cooking water.

1 Place the chick-peas in a large saucepan with water to cover. Boil for 15 minutes. Rinse and drain. Return the chick-peas to the pan. Add water to cover, 1 garlic clove, the bay leaf, 45 ml/3 tbsp of the oil and the ground pepper. Bring to the boil, then reduce the heat.

3 Sauté the bacon gently in the remaining oil with the rosemary and remaining garlic, until just golden. Discard the rosemary and garlic. Add the bacon, with its oils, to the chick-peas.

4 Add 600 ml/1 pint/2½ cups of water to the chick-peas and bring to the boil. Correct the seasoning if necessary. Reduce the heat, stir in the pasta, and cook until just tender. Serve the soup garnished with a sprig of fresh rosemary.

COOK'S TIP: Allow the soup to stand for about 10 minutes before serving to allow the flavour and texture to develop.

Herb & Chilli Gazpacho

Nutritionists recommend plenty of raw, fresh vegetables, and what better way to serve them than in this refreshing, chilled soup?

Serves 6

INGREDIENTS

1.2 kg/2½ lb ripe tomatoes
225 g/8 oz onions
2 green peppers, cored and seeded
1 green chilli, seeded
1 large cucumber
30 ml/2 tbsp red wine vinegar
15 ml/1 tbsp balsamic vinegar
30 ml/2 tbsp olive oil
1 garlic clove, crushed
300 ml/½ pint/1¼ cups tomato juice
30 ml/2 tbsp tomato purée
salt and freshly ground black pepper
30 ml/2 tbsp finely chopped mixed fresh
    herbs, plus extra to garnish
wholemeal rolls, to serve

1 Reserve about a quarter of all the fresh vegetables, except the green chilli. Roughly chop the vegetables and then place them and all the remaining ingredients in a food processor. Season to taste, then process finely. Chill the mixture in the fridge.

2 Chop all the reserved vegetables, and serve in a separate bowl to sprinkle over the soup.

3 Crush some ice cubes and add to the centre of each of six serving bowls, divide the soup among them and garnish with fresh herbs. Serve with wholemeal rolls.

Crudités with Hummus

Not just healthy, but quick and easy to prepare, home-made hummus, served with raw vegetables and a selection of breads, is always popular.

Serves 2–3

INGREDIENTS
425 g/15 oz can chick-peas, drained
30 ml/2 tbsp tahini paste
30 ml/2 tbsp fresh lemon juice
1 garlic clove, crushed
salt and freshly ground black pepper
olive oil and paprika,
    to garnish

TO SERVE
selection of salad vegetables, such as
    cucumber, chicory, baby carrots,
    pepper strips, radishes
bite-size chunks of bread, such as pitta,
    walnut, Granary, naan, bruschetta,
    or grissini sticks

1 Put the chick-peas, tahini paste, lemon juice, garlic and seasoning into a food processor or blender and process to a smooth paste.

2 Spoon the hummus into a bowl and swirl the top with the back of a spoon. Trickle over a little olive oil and sprinkle with paprika.

3 Prepare a selection of fresh salad vegetables and chunks of your favourite fresh bread or grissini sticks into finger-size pieces.

4 Set out in a colourful jumble on a large plate with the bowl of hummus in the centre. Then dip and eat!

Mushroom & Bean Pâté

A light and tasty pâté, delicious served on wholemeal bread or toast for a starter or a nutritious suppertime snack.

Serves 12

INGREDIENTS
450 g/1 lb/6 cups mushrooms, sliced
1 onion, chopped
2 garlic cloves, crushed
1 red pepper, cored, seeded and diced
30 ml/2 tbsp vegetable stock
30 ml/2 tbsp dry white wine
400 g/14 oz can red kidney beans,
    rinsed and drained
1 egg, beaten
50 g/2 oz/1 cup fresh
    wholemeal breadcrumbs
15 ml/1 tbsp chopped fresh thyme
15 ml/1 tbsp chopped fresh rosemary
salt and freshly ground black pepper
lettuce and tomatoes, to garnish
wholemeal toast, to serve

1 Preheat the oven to 180°C/350°F/ Gas 4. Grease and line a non-stick 900 g/2 lb loaf tin. Put the mushrooms, onion, garlic, red pepper, stock and wine in a pan. Cover and cook, stirring occasionally, for 10 minutes.

2 Cool slightly, then process with the beans in a blender or food processor. Transfer to a bowl. Mix in the egg, breadcrumbs, herbs and seasoning.

3 Spoon into the tin and level the surface. Bake for 45–60 minutes, until set and browned. Place on a wire rack and allow to cool completely in the tin, then refrigerate for several hours. Turn out on to a plate. Serve sliced with toast, lettuce and tomatoes.

Tuna & Bean Salad

This substantial salad is packed with proteins, vitamins, unsaturated fats and a healthy ten grams of fibre per serving.

Serves 4–6

INGREDIENTS
2 x 400 g/14 oz cans cannellini
    or borlotti beans, rinsed
    and drained
2 x 200 g/7 oz cans tuna, drained
60 ml/4 tbsp extra virgin olive oil
30 ml/2 tbsp lemon juice
15 ml/1 tbsp chopped fresh parsley
3 spring onions, thinly sliced
salt and freshly ground black pepper

1 Place the beans in a serving dish. Break the tuna into fairly large flakes and arrange over the beans.

2 In a small bowl, make the dressing by combining the oil with the lemon juice. Season with salt and pepper, and stir in the parsley. Mix well.

3 Pour the dressing over the beans and tuna. Sprinkle with the spring onions. Toss well before serving.

Cod with Lentils & Leeks

Not only do green lentils have a better flavour than red ones and hold their shape when cooked, they are also higher in dietary fibre.

Serves 4

INGREDIENTS
150 g/5 oz/⅔ cup green
   lentils, rinsed
1 bay leaf
1 garlic clove, finely chopped
grated rind of 1 orange
grated rind of 1 lemon
pinch of ground cumin
15 g/½ oz/1 tbsp butter
450 g/1 lb leeks, thinly sliced or
   cut into julienne strips
300 ml/½ pint/1¼ cups
   whipping cream
15 ml/1 tbsp lemon juice,
   or to taste
800 g/1¾ lb thick skinless cod or
   haddock fillets
salt and freshly ground
   black pepper

1 Put the lentils in a large saucepan with the bay leaf, chopped garlic and enough water to cover by 5 cm/2 in. Bring to the boil. Boil gently for 10 minutes, then reduce the heat and simmer for a further 15–30 minutes, until just tender.

> **VARIATION:** To reduce the fat content of this dish you could replace the cream with half fat crème fraîche.

2 Drain the lentils and discard the bay leaf. Stir in half the orange rind and all the lemon rind and season with cumin and salt and pepper. Transfer to a shallow ovenproof dish. Preheat the oven to 190°C/375°F/Gas 5.

3 Melt the butter in a saucepan over a medium heat. Sauté the leeks, stirring frequently, until just softened.

4 Add 250 ml/8 fl oz/1 cup of the cream and the remaining orange rind and cook gently for 15–20 minutes, until the leeks are soft and the cream has thickened. Stir in the lemon juice and season with salt and pepper.

5 Cut the fish fillets into four pieces and pull out any small bones. Season the fish with salt and pepper, place on top of the lentil mixture and press down slightly. Cover each piece of fish with a quarter of the leek mixture and pour about 15 ml/1 tbsp of the remaining cream over each.

6 Bake for about 30 minutes, until the fish is cooked through and the topping is lightly golden.

COOK'S TIP: Pulses can be cooked, drained and frozen if desired. For this recipe, thaw them before use.

Chicken & Bean Risotto

Brown rice, red kidney beans, sweetcorn and broccoli all add extra fibre to this tasty risotto. Serve as a filling lunch or supper.

Serves 4–6

INGREDIENTS

1 onion, chopped
2 garlic cloves, crushed
1 fresh red chilli, seeded and finely chopped
175 g/6 oz/2½ cups mushrooms, sliced
2 sticks celery, chopped
225 g/8 oz/generous 1 cup long grain
   brown rice
450 ml/¾ pint/scant 2 cups stock
150 ml/¼ pint/⅔ cup white wine
225 g/8 oz skinless boneless chicken
   breast, diced
400 g/14 oz can red kidney beans,
   rinsed and drained
200 g/7 oz can sweetcorn kernels, drained
115 g/4 oz/⅔ cup sultanas
175 g/6 oz small broccoli florets
30–45 ml/2–3 tbsp chopped fresh mixed herbs
salt and freshly ground black pepper

2 Stir in the chicken, kidney beans, sweetcorn and sultanas. Cook for a further 20 minutes, until almost all the liquid has been absorbed.

3 Meanwhile, cook the broccoli florets in boiling water for 5 minutes, then drain thoroughly.

VARIATION: Use 5 ml/1 tsp hot chilli powder or 2.5 ml/½ tsp chilli flakes in place of the fresh chilli, if preferred.

1 Put the onion, garlic, chilli, mushrooms, celery, rice, stock and wine in a saucepan. Cover, bring to the boil and simmer for 15 minutes.

4 Stir the broccoli florets into the risotto and add the fresh chopped herbs. Season to taste with salt and freshly ground black pepper and serve immediately.

Seven-vegetable Couscous

Couscous is made from fibre-rich semolina grains that have been rolled, dampened and coated with wheat flour.

Serves 6

INGREDIENTS
30 ml/2 tbsp sunflower or olive oil
450 g/1 lb lean lamb, cut into bite-size pieces
2 chicken breast quarters, halved
2 onions, chopped
350 g/12 oz carrots, cut into chunks
225 g/8 oz parsnips, cut into chunks
115 g/4 oz turnips, cut into cubes
6 tomatoes, peeled and chopped
900 ml/1½ pints/3¾ cups chicken stock
good pinch of ginger
1 cinnamon stick
400 g/14 oz can chick-peas, drained
400 g/14 oz/2 cups couscous
2 small courgettes, cut into julienne strips
115 g/4 oz/¾ cup French beans, trimmed and
   halved if necessary
50 g/2 oz/⅓ cup raisins
a little harissa or Tabasco sauce
salt and freshly ground black pepper

1 Heat half the oil in a large saucepan and fry the lamb, stirring frequently, until evenly browned. Transfer to a plate with a slotted spoon. Add the chicken and cook until evenly browned. Transfer to the plate with the lamb.

2 Heat the remaining oil and fry the onions over a gentle heat for 2–3 minutes. Add the carrots, parsnips and turnips. Stir, cover and cook, stirring occasionally, for 5–6 minutes.

3 Add the tomatoes, lamb, chicken and stock. Season to taste and add the ginger and cinnamon. Bring to the boil and simmer gently for 35–45 minutes, until the meat is nearly tender.

4 Skin the chick-peas by rubbing between your fingers in cold water. Discard the skins and drain. Prepare the couscous according to the instructions on the packet.

5 Add the chick-peas, courgettes, beans and raisins to the pan, stir and cook for 10–15 minutes, until the vegetables and meat are tender. Pile the couscous on a large platter, making a slight well in the centre.

6 Transfer the chicken to a plate and remove the skin and bones, if you wish. Spoon 3–4 large spoonfuls of stock into a separate pan, add harissa or Tabasco and heat gently. Return the chicken to the stew and spoon it over the couscous. Serve the sauce separately.

Toulouse Cassoulet

There are many versions of this filling and nourishing dish. This one contains lamb and pork as well as Toulouse sausages.

Serves 6–8

INGREDIENTS
450 g/1 lb/2½ cups dried white beans
  (haricot or cannellini), soaked in cold
  water, rinsed and drained
675 g/1½ lb Toulouse sausages
500 g/1¼ lb each boneless lamb
  and pork shoulder, cut into
  5 cm/2 in pieces
1 large onion, finely chopped
3–4 garlic cloves, very finely chopped
4 tomatoes, peeled, seeded
  and chopped
bouquet garni
300 ml/½ pint/1¼ cups chicken stock
60 ml/4 tbsp fresh breadcrumbs
salt and freshly ground
  black pepper

1 Put the beans in a saucepan with water to cover. Boil vigorously for 10 minutes and drain. Return to a clean pan, cover with water and bring to the boil. Reduce the heat and simmer for 45 minutes. Add a little salt and leave to soak in the cooking water.

2 Preheat the oven to 180°C/350°F/ Gas 4. Prick the sausages and cook in a large, heavy frying pan over a medium heat, turning occasionally, for 20–25 minutes, until browned. Drain on kitchen paper and pour off all but 15 ml/1 tbsp of the fat from the pan.

3 Increase the heat to medium. Season the lamb and pork and add enough to the pan to fit in one layer. Cook until browned, then transfer to a dish. Continue browning in batches.

4 Add the onion and garlic to the pan and cook, stirring, for 3–4 minutes. Stir in the tomatoes and cook for 2–3 minutes. Transfer the vegetables to the meat dish. Add the stock, bring to the boil and skim off the fat.

5 Using a slotted spoon put a quarter of the beans into a casserole. Top with a third of the sausages, vegetables and meat. Continue layering, ending with beans. Add the bouquet garni, stock and bean cooking liquid to cover.

6 Cover and bake for 2 hours (adding more bean cooking liquid if necessary). Uncover the casserole, sprinkle over the breadcrumbs and press with the back of a spoon. Cook, uncovered, for a further 20 minutes.

Beef & Vegetable Stir-fry

Stir-frying is a healthy cooking technique, which is so rapid that little oil is required and most of the nutrients are retained.

Serves 4

INGREDIENTS

10–15 ml/2–3 tsp chilli powder
5 ml/1 tsp ground cumin
2.5 ml/½ tsp dried oregano
450 g/1 lb topside of beef, cut into
    thin strips
30 ml/2 tbsp vegetable oil
5 spring onions, cut diagonally into
    2.5 cm/1 in lengths
1 small green pepper, cored, seeded and
    thinly sliced
1 small red pepper, cored, seeded and
    thinly sliced
1 small yellow pepper, cored, seeded
    and thinly sliced
115 g/4 oz baby corn cobs, halved
    lengthways, or 225 g/8 oz canned
    sweetcorn, drained
4 garlic cloves, crushed
30 ml/2 tbsp lime or lemon juice
30 ml/2 tbsp chopped
    fresh coriander
salt and freshly ground black pepper

VARIATION: This recipe would also work well using thinly sliced, skinless chicken breast or lean pork fillet.

1 In a medium bowl, combine the spices, oregano and a little salt and pepper. Rub the mixture into the beef strips to coat evenly.

2 Heat half the oil in a wok or frying pan over a high heat. Add the beef and stir-fry for 3–4 minutes, until well browned. Remove the beef from the wok with a slotted spoon and keep hot.

3 Heat the remaining vegetable oil in the wok and stir-fry the spring onions, peppers, corn cobs and garlic for about 3 minutes, until just tender.

4 Cover with a second layer of leaves and mushroom barley filling. Continue until the centre is full. Draw together opposite corners of the muslin and tie firmly. Set the steaming basket in a saucepan containing 2.5 cm/1 in of simmering water, cover and steam for 30 minutes.

5 To serve, place on a warmed serving plate, untie the muslin and carefully pull it away from underneath the stuffed cabbage.

COOK'S TIP: A range of nut butters is available in all leading health food stores.

Tagliatelle with Tomato & Courgette Sauce

As well as being an excellent source of dietary fibre and rich in complex carbohydrates, pasta is immensely versatile and easy to prepare.

Serves 3–4

INGREDIENTS
225 g/8 oz wholewheat tagliatelle
30 ml/2 tbsp olive oil
1 onion, chopped
2 celery sticks, chopped
1 garlic clove, crushed
2 courgettes, halved lengthways
   and sliced
5–6 ripe tomatoes, peeled and
   roughly chopped
30 ml/2 tbsp sun-dried
   tomato paste
50 g/2 oz/½ cup flaked
   almonds, toasted
salt and freshly ground
   black pepper

1 Bring a large saucepan of lightly salted water to the boil, add the pasta and cook for about 12 minutes (or according to the instructions on the packet), until just tender.

COOK'S TIP: If using fresh pasta, you'll need double the quantity, i.e. 450 g/1 lb for 3-4 hearty appetites. Fresh tagliatelle usually only takes 3–4 minutes to cook and is ready when it's tender but still *al dente*.

2 Meanwhile, heat the oil in another pan and add the onion, celery, garlic and courgettes. Sauté over a gentle heat for 3–4 minutes, or until the onions are softened and lightly browned.

3 Stir in the tomatoes and sun-dried tomato paste. Cook gently for 5 minutes more, then add salt and pepper to taste.

4 Drain the pasta, return it to the pan and add the sauce. Toss well. Place in a warmed serving dish, scatter the toasted almonds over the top and serve immediately.

Greek Stuffed Vegetables

Vegetables stuffed with a savoury filling of rice, nuts, dried fruit, vegetables and herbs are a nutritionally well-balanced and scrumptious vegetarian main course. The filling also makes a delicious salad.

Serves 3–6

INGREDIENTS
1 medium aubergine
2 large tomatoes
1 large onion, chopped
2 garlic cloves, crushed
45 ml/3 tbsp olive oil
200 g/7 oz/1 cup brown rice
600 ml/1 pint/2½ cups
   vegetable stock
75 g/3 oz/½ cup pine nuts
50 g/2 oz/¼ cup currants
45 ml/3 tbsp fresh dill, chopped
45 ml/3 tbsp fresh parsley, chopped
15 ml/1 tbsp fresh mint, chopped
1 large green pepper, halved,
   cored and seeded
extra olive oil, to sprinkle
salt and freshly ground black pepper
Greek-style yogurt and fresh sprigs of dill,
   to garnish

1 Halve the aubergine, scoop out the flesh, leaving a thin shell, and chop the flesh finely. Salt the insides of the aubergine shells and leave upside down for 20 minutes while you prepare the other ingredients.

2 Cut the tops from the tomatoes and scoop out the flesh. Roughly chop the flesh and the tomato tops, and set aside.

3 Fry the onion, garlic and chopped aubergine in the oil for 10 minutes, then stir in the rice and cook for 2 minutes. Add the tomato flesh, stock, pine nuts, currants and seasoning. Bring to the boil, cover and simmer for 25–30 minutes until the rice is tender, then stir in the fresh herbs.

4 Preheat the oven to 190°C/375°F/Gas 5. Brush an ovenproof dish with oil. Blanch the aubergine and green pepper halves in boiling water for about 3 minutes, then drain them upside down.

5 Spoon the rice filling into the vegetable 'containers' and place in the dish. Drizzle some olive oil over the stuffed vegetables. Bake for 25–30 minutes. Serve hot, with spoonfuls of yogurt and dill sprigs.

Courgette & Sweetcorn Pizza

This tasty wholewheat pizza can be served hot or cold with a mixed bean salad and fresh, crusty bread or baked potatoes.

Serves 6

INGREDIENTS
225 g/8 oz/2 cups plain wholemeal flour
10 ml/2 tsp baking powder
50 g/2 oz/4 tbsp margarine
150 ml/¼ pint/⅔ cup milk
30 ml/2 tbsp tomato purée
10 ml/2 tsp dried herbes de Provence
10 ml/2 tsp olive oil
1 onion, sliced
1 garlic clove, crushed
2 small courgettes, sliced
115 g/4 oz/1⅔ cups mushrooms, sliced
115 g/4 oz/¾ cup frozen sweetcorn kernels
2 plum tomatoes, sliced
50 g/2 oz/½ cup red Leicester cheese,
   finely grated
50 g/2 oz/½ cup Mozzarella cheese,
   finely grated
salt and freshly ground black pepper
basil sprigs, to garnish

1 Preheat the oven to 220°C/425°F/ Gas 7. Line a baking sheet with non-stick baking paper, if necessary. Put the flour, a pinch of salt and the baking powder in a bowl and rub the margarine lightly into the flour until the mixture resembles breadcrumbs.

2 Add enough milk to form a soft dough and knead lightly. On a lightly floured surface, roll out the dough to a round 25 cm/10 in in diameter.

3 Place the dough on the baking sheet and make the edges slightly thicker than the centre. Spread the tomato purée over the base and sprinkle the herbs on top.

4 Heat the oil in a frying pan, add the onion, garlic, courgettes and mushrooms and cook gently, stirring occasionally, for 10 minutes.

5 Spread the vegetable mixture over the pizza base and sprinkle over the sweetcorn and seasoning. Arrange the tomato slices on top.

6 Mix together the cheeses and sprinkle over the pizza. Bake for 25–30 minutes, until cooked and golden brown. Serve hot or cold in slices, garnished with basil sprigs.

VARIATION: Try this quick base with other toppings such as baby corn cobs, cooked beans, cherry tomatoes or crumbled goat's cheese.

Parsnip, Aubergine & Cashew Biryani

Parsnips have a higher fibre content than almost any other vegetable and here they are combined with aubergine and nuts in an unusual biryani.

Serves 4–6

INGREDIENTS
1 small aubergine, sliced
3 parsnips, peeled and cored
3 onions
2 garlic cloves
2.5 cm/1 in piece fresh root ginger
about 60 ml/4 tbsp vegetable oil
175 g/6 oz/1 cup unsalted
    cashew nuts
40 g/1½ oz/¼ cup sultanas
1 red pepper, cored, seeded
    and sliced
5 ml/1 tsp ground cumin
5 ml/1 tsp ground coriander
2.5 ml/½ tsp chilli powder
120 ml/4 fl oz/½ cup natural yogurt
300 ml/½ pint/1¼ cups vegetable stock
275 g/10 oz/1½ cups basmati rice, soaked in
    cold water for 40 minutes
25 g/1 oz/2 tbsp butter
salt and freshly ground black pepper
sprigs of coriander and 2 hard-boiled eggs,
    quartered, to garnish

1 Sprinkle the aubergine with salt and leave for 30 minutes. Rinse, pat dry and dice. Dice the parsnips. Chop 1 onion and put in a food processor or blender with the garlic and ginger. Add 30–45 ml/2–3 tbsp water and process to a paste.

2 Finely slice the remaining onions. Heat 45 ml/3 tbsp of the oil and fry gently for 10–15 minutes, until deep golden brown. Remove and drain. Add 40 g/1½ oz/¼ cup of the cashew nuts to the pan and stir-fry for 2 minutes. Add the sultanas and fry until they swell. Remove and drain.

3 Add the diced aubergine and sliced pepper to the pan and stir-fry for 4–5 minutes. Drain on kitchen paper. Fry the parsnips for 4–5 minutes. Stir in the remaining cashew nuts and fry for 1 minute. Transfer to the plate with the aubergines.

4 Add the remaining oil to the pan. Add the onion paste. Cook, stirring, over a moderate heat for 4–5 minutes, until golden. Stir in the cumin, coriander and chilli powder. Cook, stirring, for 1 minute. Reduce the heat and add the yogurt.

5 Bring the mixture to the boil and stir in the stock, parsnips, aubergines and peppers. Season, cover and simmer for 30–40 minutes, until the parsnips are tender, then transfer to a casserole. Preheat the oven to 150°C/300°F/ Gas 2.

6 Drain the rice and add to 300 ml/ ½ pint/1¼ cups salted boiling water. Cook for 5–6 minutes.

7 Drain, then pile on top of the parsnips. Using the handle of a wooden spoon, make a hole through the rice. Scatter the reserved fried onions, nuts and sultanas over the rice and dot with butter. Cover with a double layer of foil and a lid. Cook in the oven for 35–40 minutes. Serve garnished with coriander and eggs.

Savoury Nut Loaf

Packed with goodness, this delicious nut loaf makes a marvellous summer lunch or perfect picnic food.

Serves 8

INGREDIENTS

15 ml/1 tbsp olive oil, plus extra
    for greasing
1 onion, chopped
1 leek, chopped
2 celery sticks, finely chopped
225 g/8 oz/3 cups mushrooms, chopped
2 garlic cloves, crushed
425 g/15 oz can green lentils, rinsed
    and drained
115 g/4 oz/1 cup mixed nuts, such as
    hazelnuts, cashew nuts and brazils,
    finely chopped
50 g/2 oz/½ cup wholemeal flour
50 g/2 oz/½ cup grated mature
    Cheddar cheese
1 egg, beaten
45–60 ml/3–4 tbsp chopped fresh
    mixed herbs
salt and freshly ground black pepper
flat leaf parsley sprigs and chives,
    to garnish

1 Preheat the oven to 190°C/375°F/ Gas 5. Lightly grease and line the base and sides of a 900 g/2 lb loaf tin.

COOK'S TIP: If preferred, use 150 g/5 oz dried lentils. Wash the lentils, place in a pan, cover with water and cook for 30–45 minutes until tender.

2 Heat the oil in a large saucepan. Add the onion, leek, celery, mushrooms and garlic and cook gently, stirring occasionally, for 10 minutes, until the vegetables have softened.

3 Add the lentils, nuts, flour, cheese, egg and herbs to the pan. Season with salt and pepper and mix thoroughly.

4 Spoon the mixture into the prepared loaf tin and level the surface. Bake, uncovered, for 50–60 minutes, or until the loaf is lightly browned on top and firm to the touch.

5 Cool the loaf slightly in the tin, then turn it out on to a large serving plate and remove the paper. Serve hot or cold, cut into slices, and garnished with flat leaf parsley sprigs and chives.

VARIATION: You can vary the flavour of this loaf by using grated carrot instead of the leek, brown lentils and a smoked cheese.

Vegetarian Fried Noodles

Leaving vegetables unpeeled whenever possible not only increases the quantity of fibre but also helps to preserve their vitamins and minerals.

Serves 4

INGREDIENTS

2 eggs
5 ml/1 tsp chilli powder
5 ml/1 tsp turmeric
60 ml/4 tbsp vegetable oil
1 large onion, finely sliced
2 red chillies, seeded and finely sliced
15 ml/1 tbsp soy sauce
2 large unpeeled cooked potatoes, cut into small cubes
1 block tofu, sliced
225 g/8 oz/1 cup beansprouts
115 g/4 oz/¾ cup green beans, blanched
350 g/12 oz fresh thick egg noodles
salt and freshly ground black pepper
sliced spring onions, to garnish

1 Beat the eggs lightly, then strain them into a bowl. Heat a lightly greased omelette pan. Pour in half of the egg to cover the bottom of the pan thinly. When the egg is just set, turn the omelette over and fry the other side briefly.

2 Slide on to a plate, blot with kitchen paper, roll up and cut into narrow strips. Make a second omelette, and slice. Set aside.

3 In a cup, mix together the chilli powder and turmeric. Form a paste by stirring in a little water. Heat the oil in a wok or large frying pan. Fry the onion until soft. Reduce the heat and add the chilli paste, sliced chillies and soy sauce. Fry for 2–3 minutes.

4 Add the potatoes and tofu and fry for about 2 minutes, mixing well with the chillies. Add the beansprouts, green beans and noodles.

5 Gently stir-fry until the noodles are evenly coated and heated through. Season with salt and pepper. Serve hot, garnished with the omelette strips and spring onion slices.

Courgette & Dill Tart

Although enriched with cream, this special-occasion tart is also nutritious and high in fibre.

Serves 4

INGREDIENTS
115 g/4 oz/1 cup plain wholemeal flour
115 g/4 oz/1 cup self-raising flour
115 g/4 oz/½ cup unsalted butter, chilled
  and diced
75 ml/5 tbsp ice-cold water
salt

FOR THE FILLING
15 ml/1 tbsp sunflower oil
3 courgettes, thinly sliced
2 egg yolks
150 ml/¼ pint/⅔ cup
  double cream
1 garlic clove, crushed
15 ml/1 tbsp finely chopped
  fresh dill, plus a sprig, to garnish
salt and freshly ground
  black pepper

1 Sift the flours into a bowl, returning any of the wheat bran to the bowl, then place in a food processor. Add a pinch of salt and the diced butter and process using the pulse button until the mixture resembles fine breadcrumbs.

2 Gradually add the water until the mixture forms a dough. Do not over-process. Rest the pastry by wrapping it in clear film and placing it in the fridge for 30 minutes.

3 Preheat the oven to 200°C/400°F/ Gas 6 and grease a 20 cm/8 in flan tin. Roll out the pastry and ease into the tin. Prick the base with a fork and bake "blind" for 10–15 minutes, until lightly browned.

4 Meanwhile, heat the oil in a frying pan and sauté the courgettes for 2–3 minutes, turning occasionally, until lightly browned. Blend the egg yolks, double cream, garlic and chopped dill in a small bowl. Season to taste with salt and pepper.

5 Line the pastry case with layers of courgette and gently pour over the cream mixture. Return to the oven for 25–30 minutes, or until the filling is firm and lightly golden. Cool in the tin and then remove and serve garnished with the dill sprig.

Black-eyed Bean Stew with Spicy Pumpkin

This unusual dish of lightly spiced pumpkin and black-eyed beans provides a superb combination of both fibre content and flavour.

Serves 3–4

INGREDIENTS
225 g/8 oz/1¼ cups black-eyed beans,
   soaked in cold water and drained
1 onion, chopped
1 green or red pepper, cored,
   seeded and chopped
2 garlic cloves, chopped
1 vegetable stock cube
1 thyme sprig or 5 ml/1 tsp dried thyme
5 ml/1 tsp paprika
2.5 ml/½ tsp mixed spice
2 carrots, sliced
15–30 ml/1–2 tbsp palm or groundnut oil
salt and hot pepper sauce

FOR THE SPICY PUMPKIN
675 g/1½ lb pumpkin
1 onion
25 g/1 oz/2 tbsp butter or margarine
2 garlic cloves, crushed
3 tomatoes, peeled and chopped
2.5 ml/½ tsp ground cinnamon
10 ml/2 tsp curry powder
pinch of freshly grated nutmeg
300 ml/½ pint/1¼ cups water
salt, hot pepper sauce and freshly
   ground black pepper

1 Place the black-eyed beans in a pan, cover generously with water and bring to the boil.

2 Add the onion, green or red pepper, garlic, stock cube, thyme and spices. Simmer for 45 minutes, or until the beans are just tender. Season to taste with salt and a little hot pepper sauce.

3 Add the carrots and palm or groundnut oil and continue cooking for about 10–12 minutes, until the carrots are cooked, adding a little more water if necessary. Remove from the heat and set aside.

4 To make the spicy pumpkin, cut the pumpkin into cubes and finely chop the onion.

COOK'S TIP: Pumpkins are tasty and versatile. Available in late summer, they can be kept until spring if stored in a cool, dry place.

5 Melt the butter or margarine in a frying pan or saucepan, and add the pumpkin, onion, garlic, tomatoes, spices and water. Stir well to combine, and simmer until the pumpkin is soft. Season with salt, hot pepper sauce and black pepper to taste. Serve with the black-eyed beans.

Brussels Sprouts with Chestnuts

This classic combination is healthy and tastes wonderful.

Serves 6

INGREDIENTS
450 g/1 lb Brussels sprouts, trimmed
115 g/4 oz/½ cup butter
3 celery sticks, cut diagonally in
 1 cm/½ in lengths
1 large onion, thinly sliced
400 g/14 oz can whole chestnuts in brine,
 drained and rinsed
1.5 ml/¼ tsp grated nutmeg
grated rind of 1 lemon
salt and freshly ground black pepper

1 Cook the Brussels sprouts in a pan of boiling salted water for 3–4 minutes. Drain well.

2 Melt the butter in a frying pan over a low heat. Add the celery and onion and cook for 5 minutes, until softened.

3 Raise the heat to medium and add the chestnuts and sprouts. Stir in the nutmeg and salt and pepper to taste. Cook, stirring frequently, for about 2 minutes until hot.

4 Stir in the grated lemon rind. Transfer to a warmed serving dish and serve immediately.

Green Peas & Baby Onions

Peas are an excellent source of fibre and are delicious with baby onions.

Serves 6

INGREDIENTS
15 g/½ oz/1 tbsp butter
12 baby onions, peeled
1 small butterhead lettuce, shredded
275 g/10 oz/2½ cups shelled fresh green peas
 or frozen peas, thawed
5 ml/1 tsp sugar
30 ml/2 tbsp water
2 sprigs mint
salt and freshly ground black pepper

1 Melt the butter in a frying pan. Add the onions and cook over medium heat for about 10 minutes, until they just begin to colour.

2 Add the lettuce, peas, sugar and water. Season with salt and pepper. Bring to the boil. Reduce the heat to low, cover and simmer, stirring occasionally, until the peas are tender, about 15 minutes for fresh peas and 10 minutes for frozen peas.

3 Strip the mint leaves from the stems. Chop finely with a sharp knife. Stir the mint into the peas and serve.

Right: Brussels Sprouts (top); Green Peas

Cabbage Slaw with Date & Apple

The maximum amount of vitamin C is retained in this crunchy salad.

Serves 6–8

INGREDIENTS
¼ small white cabbage
¼ small red cabbage
¼ small Savoy cabbage
175 g/6 oz/1 cup dried stoned dates
3 eating apples
juice of 1 lemon
10 ml/2 tsp caraway seeds

FOR THE DRESSING
60 ml/4 tbsp olive oil
15 ml/1 tbsp cider vinegar
5 ml/1 tsp clear honey
salt and freshly ground black pepper

1 Finely shred all the cabbages and place them in a large salad bowl. Chop the dates and add them to the cabbage. Core the eating apples, without peeling, and chop them into a mixing bowl. Add the lemon juice and toss together to prevent discoloration before adding to the salad bowl.

2 Make the dressing. Combine the oil, vinegar, honey and seasoning in a screw-top jar, then shake well. Toss the salad in the dressing, sprinkle with the caraway seeds, toss again and serve.

Sprouted Seed Salad

Sprouted beans and seeds have a high vitamin and mineral content.

Serves 4

INGREDIENTS
2 eating apples
115 g/4 oz/⅓ cup alfalfa sprouts
115 g/4 oz/½ cup beansprouts
115 g/4 oz/½ cup aduki bean sprouts
¼ cucumber, sliced
1 bunch watercress, trimmed
1 carton mustard and cress, trimmed

FOR THE DRESSING
150 ml/¼ pint/⅔ cup natural yogurt
juice of ½ lemon
bunch of chives, snipped
30 ml/2 tbsp chopped fresh herbs
freshly ground black pepper

1 Core and slice the apples, but do not peel. Mix together the apples, sprouts, cucumber, watercress and mustard and cress in a large bowl.

2 Beat together the yogurt and lemon juice in a jug until thoroughly combined. Stir in the chives and herbs and season with pepper to taste. Drizzle over the salad and toss together just before serving.

Right: Cabbage Slaw (top); Seed Salad

Cracked Wheat Salad with Walnuts & Herbs

Cracked wheat, also known as bulgur wheat, has been processed only to the extent that the grains are cracked so that they readily absorb moisture.

Serves 4

INGREDIENTS

225 g/8 oz/1¼ cups
    cracked wheat
350 ml/12 fl oz/1½ cups vegetable stock
1 cinnamon stick
generous pinch of ground cumin
pinch of cayenne pepper
pinch of ground cloves
5 ml/1 tsp salt
10 mangetouts, topped and tailed
1 red and 1 yellow pepper, roasted, skinned,
    seeded and diced
2 plum tomatoes, peeled, seeded
    and diced
2 shallots, finely sliced
5 black olives, stoned and cut
    into quarters
30 ml/2 tbsp each shredded fresh basil,
    mint and parsley
30 ml/2 tbsp roughly chopped walnuts
30 ml/2 tbsp balsamic vinegar
120 ml/4 fl oz/½ cup extra virgin
    olive oil
freshly ground black pepper
onion rings, to garnish

1 Place the cracked wheat in a large bowl. Pour the vegetable stock into a saucepan and bring to the boil with the spices and salt.

2 Cook for 1 minute, then pour the stock over the cracked wheat and leave to stand for 30 minutes.

3 In another bowl, mix together the mangetouts, peppers, tomatoes, shallots, olives, herbs and walnuts. Add the vinegar, olive oil and a little black pepper and stir thoroughly to mix.

COOK'S TIP: To roast the peppers, cut in half and place skin side up on a baking tray. Place in an oven preheated to 220°C/425°F/Gas 7 and roast for about 20 minutes, until charred. Transfer to a plastic bag, knot it and leave for 10 minutes. The skin can then be pulled away.

4 Strain the cracked wheat of any liquid and discard the cinnamon stick. Place in a serving bowl, stir in the fresh vegetable mixture and serve, garnished with onion rings.

Baked Stuffed Apples

This is an especially good way to cook apples as both the flavour and nutrients remain locked inside them.

Serves 4

INGREDIENTS
4 large cooking apples
75 g/3 oz/scant ½ cup light
    muscovado sugar
75 g/3 oz/⅓ cup butter, softened
grated rind and juice
    of ½ orange
1.5 ml/¼ tsp ground cinnamon
30 ml/2 tbsp crushed
    ratafia biscuits
50 g/2 oz/½ cup pecan
    nuts, chopped
50 g/2 oz/⅓ cup luxury mixed
    glacé fruit, chopped

1 Preheat the oven to 180°C/350°F/ Gas 4. Remove the apple cores, then double each core cavity by shaving off more flesh with a corer. Score each apple around its equator, using a knife. Stand the apples in an ovenproof dish.

2 Mix together the sugar, butter, orange rind and juice, cinnamon and ratafia crumbs. Beat well, then stir in the nuts and glacé fruit.

3 Divide the filling among the apples, piling it high. Shield the filling with a small piece of foil. Bake the apples for 45–60 minutes, until they are tender.

Papaya Baked with Ginger

Besides being delicious, papaya aids digestion, so this is the ideal dessert to serve at the end of a substantial meal.

Serves 4

INGREDIENTS

2 ripe papayas
2 pieces stem ginger in syrup, drained,
    plus 15 ml/1 tbsp syrup from the jar
8 amaretti or other dessert biscuits,
    coarsely crushed
45 ml/3 tbsp raisins
shredded, finely pared rind and juice
    of 1 lime
25 g/1 oz/¼ cup pistachio
    nuts, chopped
15 ml/1 tbsp light muscovado sugar
60 ml/4 tbsp crème fraîche,
    plus extra to serve

1 Preheat the oven to 200°C/400°F/ Gas 6. Cut the papayas in half and scoop out their seeds. Place the halves in an ovenproof dish and set aside. Cut the stem ginger into fine matchsticks.

2 Combine the crushed biscuits, stem ginger and raisins in a bowl. Mix in the lime rind and juice, two-thirds of the nuts, the sugar and the crème fraîche.

3 Fill the papaya halves and drizzle with the syrup. Sprinkle with the remaining nuts. Bake for 25 minutes, or until tender. Serve with crème fraîche.

Pineapple & Peach Upside-down Pudding

A tasty combination of pineapple and peaches. Serve this old favourite with low fat custard or ice cream for a really healthy dessert.

Serves 6

INGREDIENTS
75 ml/5 tbsp golden syrup
225 g/8 oz can pineapple cubes in fruit juice
175 g/6 oz/¾ cup ready-to-eat dried peaches, chopped
115 g/4 oz/generous ½ cup caster sugar
115 g/4 oz/8 tbsp half fat spread
175 g/6 oz/1½ cups self-raising wholemeal flour
5 ml/1 tsp baking powder
2 eggs

1 Preheat the oven to 180°C/350°F/Gas 4. Lightly grease an 18 cm/7 in loose-based round cake tin and line the base with non-stick baking paper.

2 Heat the golden syrup gently in a saucepan until runny and pour over the base of the prepared tin, turning the tin to cover the base completely.

3 Strain the pineapple, reserving 45 ml/3 tbsp of the juice. Mix together the pineapple and peaches and scatter them over the syrup layer.

4 Put the caster sugar, half fat spread, flour, baking powder, eggs and reserved pineapple juice in a bowl and beat together until smooth.

5 Spread the cake mixture evenly over the fruit and level the surface. Bake for about 45 minutes, until risen and golden brown. Turn out carefully on to a serving plate and serve hot or cold in slices.

VARIATION: Other combinations of canned and dried fruit work just as well, such as apricots and pears or peaches and figs.

Carrot & Coconut Cake

This satisfying cake, made with a delicious combination of flavours, makes a healthy snack with morning coffee.

Serves 10

INGREDIENTS
115 g/4 oz/½ cup half fat spread
115 g/4 oz/generous ½ cup caster sugar
2 eggs
175 g/6 oz/1½ cups self-raising wholemeal
    flour, sifted
50 g/2 oz/3 cups bran
5 ml/1 tsp baking powder, sifted
about 90 ml/6 tbsp skimmed milk
225 g/8 oz/1⅔ cups carrots,
    coarsely grated
115 g/4 oz/1¼ cups desiccated coconut
50 g/2 oz/⅓ cup sultanas
finely grated rind of 1 orange
15–30 ml/1–2 tbsp golden granulated sugar,
    to sprinkle

2 Fold in the grated carrots, desiccated coconut, sultanas, orange rind and extra milk if needed, to make a soft dropping consistency.

1 Preheat the oven to 180°C/350°F/ Gas 4. Lightly grease a deep 18 cm/ 7 in round cake tin and line with non-stick baking paper. Put the half fat spread, caster sugar, eggs, flour, bran, baking powder and milk in a bowl and beat together until thoroughly mixed.

3 Spoon the mixture into the prepared tin and level the surface with a palette knife.

VARIATION: If you are gradually introducing fibre into your diet, you could replace the bran in this recipe with 50 g/2 oz/½ cup self-raising wholemeal flour.

4 Sprinkle the top with granulated sugar and bake for about 1 hour, until risen, golden brown and firm to the touch. Cool in the tin for a few minutes, then turn out on to a wire rack to cool completely. Serve in slices.

Wholemeal Apple, Apricot & Walnut Loaf

Cut a slice of this fruity loaf for a healthy snack whenever you feel your energy beginning to flag.

Makes 10–12 slices

INGREDIENTS
225 g/8 oz/2 cups plain
    wholemeal flour
5 ml/1 tsp baking powder
pinch of salt
115 g/4 oz/½ cup sunflower margarine
175 g/6 oz/¾ cup soft light
    brown sugar
2 eggs, lightly beaten
grated rind and juice of
    1 orange
50 g/2 oz/½ cup chopped walnuts
50 g/2 oz/¼ cup ready-to-eat dried
    apricots, chopped
1 large cooking apple
oil, for greasing

1 Preheat the oven to 180°C/350°F/ Gas 4. Line and grease a 900 g/2 lb loaf tin with non-stick baking paper.

2 Sift the flour, baking powder and salt into a large mixing bowl, then tip the bran remaining in the sieve into the mixture. Add the margarine, sugar, eggs, orange rind and juice. Stir, then beat with a hand-held electric beater until smooth.

3 Stir in the chopped walnuts and apricots. Quarter, peel and core the cooking apple, chop it roughly and add it to the mixture. Stir to incorporate all the ingredients, then spoon the mixture into the prepared tin and level the top.

4 Bake for 1 hour, or until a skewer inserted into the centre of the loaf comes out clean. Cool in the tin for about 5 minutes, then turn the loaf out on to a wire rack and peel off the lining paper. Leave to cool completely. When cold, store the loaf in an airtight tin.

Fruity Muesli Bars

These fruity muesli bars make an appetizing, high fibre and nourishing treat for a take–away snack.

Makes 10–12

INGREDIENTS
115 g/4 oz/½ cup half fat spread,
    plus extra for greasing
75 g/3 oz/scant ½ cup soft light
    brown sugar
45 ml/3 tbsp golden syrup
150 g/5 oz/1¼ cups no-added sugar
    Swiss-style muesli
50 g/2 oz/½ cup rolled oats
5 ml/1 tsp ground mixed spice
50 g/2 oz/⅓ cup sultanas
50 g/2 oz/⅓ cup ready-to-eat dried
    pears, chopped

1 Preheat the oven to 180°C/350°F/ Gas 4. Lightly grease an 18 cm/7 in square cake tin.

2 Put the half fat spread, sugar and golden syrup in a saucepan and gently heat, stirring constantly, until melted and blended.

3 Remove the pan from the heat, add the muesli, rolled oats, mixed spice, sultanas and chopped pears and mix together thoroughly.

4 Transfer the mixture to the prepared cake tin and level the surface, pressing down firmly with the back of a spoon.

5 Bake for 20–30 minutes, until golden brown. Cool for a few minutes in the tin, then mark into 10 to 12 bars using a sharp knife. Leave to firm up.

6 When firm to the touch, remove the muesli bars from the tin with a palette knife and place on a wire rack to cool completely. The bars can be stored in an airtight tin for several days.

VARIATION: A combination of rolled oats and oatmeal can be used in place of muesli for a delicious change. Or you could use chopped nuts, raisins and oats. Grind the nuts if the bars are for young children.

Index

First published in 1999 by Lorenz Books © Anness Publishing Limited 1999

Lorenz Books is an imprint of Anness Publishing Limited, Hermes House, 88–89 Blackfriars Road, London SE1 8HA

This edition distributed in Canada by Raincoast Books, 8680 Cambie Street, Vancouver, British Columbia, V6P 6M9

ISBN 0 7548 0318 X

A CIP catalogue record for this book is available from the British Library.

Publisher: Joanna Lorenz
Editor: Valerie Ferguson
Series Designer: Bobbie Colgate Stone
Designer: Andrew Heath
Production Controller: Joanna King

Recipes contributed by: Carla Capalbo, Kit Chan, Maxine Clark, Frances Cleary, Carole Clements, Roz Denny, Patrizia Diemling, Rosamund Grant, Rebekah Hassan, Christine Ingram, Maggie Mayhew, Maggie Pannell, Katherine Richmond, Anne Sheasby, Steven Wheeler, Elizabeth Wolf-Cohen.

Photography: William Adams-Lingwood, Karl Adamson, Edward Allwright, James Duncan, John Freeman, Michelle Garrett, Amanda Heywood, David Jordan, Patrick McLeavey, Michael Michaels, Thomas Odulate.

1 3 5 7 9 10 8 6 4 2

The information presented in the table on page 7 has been compiled from McCance and Widdowson's The Composition of Foods, 5th edition and relevant supplements. Data is reproduced with the kind permission of The Royal Society of Chemistry and Controller of Her Majesty's Stationery Office.

Notes:
For all recipes, quantities are given in both metric and imperial measures and, where appropriate, measures are also given in standard cups and spoons. Follow one set, but not a mixture, because they are not interchangeable.

Standard spoon and cup measures are level.

1 tsp = 5 ml   1 tbsp = 15 ml   1 cup = 250 ml/8 fl oz

Australian standard tablespoons are 20 ml. Australian readers should use 3 tsp in place of 1 tbsp for measuring small quantities of gelatine, cornflour, salt, etc.

Medium eggs are used unless otherwise stated.

Printed and bound in Singapore